Waldeinsamke

Liam Porter

Published by Nine Pens
2021
www.ninepens.co.uk

The right of the author to be identified as the author of this
work has been asserted by their accordance with the
Copyright, Designs and Patents act 1988

ISBN: 978-1-8384321-5-7

006

For Jessica, Erik, Mum, & Dad.

For a time / I rest in the grace of the world, and am free.

- Wendell Berry

Contents

Nightfall at the Jetty

- for Wendell Berry

I come not for answers
nor am I foreshadowed by grief

I am here simply to listen
to the river song & robin.

Strange how they hide
when granted no thought

how they wait for the gap
in the wood pigeon's call

like the gap between heartbeats
when man's presence is no more

& in whose absence
the world lifts into applause:

splash of mallard, whisper of oak
& in the moment before return

a ghost-white owl
cutting the purple dusk in two.

A Blessing

to sit aside
the jetty
in the later
days of an
English spring,
the River Dee
dreaming past,
splash of oar,
Africa by Toto
playing from
the bluetooth
speaker of
drunken youths
who idle by
in a blow up
canoe as an
older man
with canvas
& easel
paints the
Georgian
houses atop
the bank.

I wait for J.

It has been
three months
- long weeks of
sight contained
within square
of white wall
& bright screen.

But here,
the eye stretches
as far as it needs,
& scanning
the vast expanse
of a world
resumed,
the wait
is over, for
she appears,
bright smile,
hair curled
in the heat,
a bottle of red
in her hand.

Waldeinsamkeit

- translation: the feeling of being alone in the woods

There is no map to this forest yet you stand at its edge,
whisper your way past nettle-bush, hemlock, silver birch,
into a silence thick & loud, a pressure that builds like leaf-bed.

There are dens here: skeletal & rotten, all ash & cut-root,
cicatrix upon the skin of beech & oak

& yet this does not warn you off, rather, welcomes you in,
for there must have been heat here, the dancing of wildfire.

Read these clues & continue. Hear whispers slip
through the canopy, single strings of sunrise hinting
that this shadowed woodland could soon turn to glade

where for once the dark won't draw in & the clarity of light
won't be too much or too soon

where at your feet, the beaten path opens up into foxglove,
honeysuckle, bluebell.

A Thievery of Youth

Perhaps the hole is only wide enough
for this small boy's hand

the branch able to take
no more than his weight

because it's solely a body this innocent
who could hold a world in his palm

& not recognising mistake or repercussion,
take home this blue specked egg,

feel the shell cool & harden
as it is placed between his socks.

Later, when the world is turned off:
a snap & crack from the dark

& somehow pushing open the drawer,
a chick, furless & twisted,

drags its limp self across the floor,
beak scratching the laminate,

& in a first or final call for a mother,
a shrill cry slashing the night in half.

School of Dance

Featherweight leg held straight
& toes pointed to the floor

his feet kiss the ground as he skips,
pirouettes, turns & bows to the parents.

Isn't he marvellous, they cry
from cheap cafe tables

all beams & clapped hands
for his straight-back & robin-chest.

I sip my tea. It burns, tastes of violence,
of all boy secondary schools

where muscles appear
at the same time as anger.

Ay *Ginge, Faggot*, I shout,
& now it is me who kicks

& his red & purple leotard
turns to skin, bruised & bent,

curled on the schoolyard.

Counter Attack

based on the Urban Goals photography set by Michael Kirkham.

Their goals are bricked up, or rather, made of brick,
posts & crossbar spray-painted white.

Their stadium is the street outside the boarded up
local boozer, shadowed by high-rise council block.

They sprint in last season's kit to fans & flags at the curb,
a pile-on of skinny limbs, shinpads, socks pulled to the knee.

Here, the *no* in *no ball games* is crossed out
& armed only with paint & a ball & a game

the boys have turned the wall into a revolution,
a canvas of hope, a white painted promise of escape.

High On Mountaintop

The criticism was because they had to call out the rescue team
who arrived in full strength – mountain ambulance,
rescue dog & helicopter – for these three, jelly-legged
& white-faced at the summit.

Their equipment was not Gore-Tex jacket, carabiner or pair of
hiking boots but a packet of king size Rizlas, a pouch of
Amber Leaf & a large amount of something else.

Think of the moment before paranoia set in, when the cloud
broke into sun & blue sky, revealed the great Wast Water
lake, rolling hills, patchwork farmland, power stations & the
glint of cars bumper to bumper on a rush-hour A595.

Think of the moment, these boys, having escaped
& found their high at the peak of Scafell Pike, shouted
either to each other or to nobody in particular

This is it lads! This. Is. It.

Portrait of Mountain as Therapist

Snowdon, all grey, cloud-covered
right up to the final hundred metres
where I break through & a sea
of cotton wool, slow-floating at my feet
spreads to the sky's horizon.

Here, all is blue & sunshine, silence
the clearest it has ever been, different
to other types of quiet, say, that of a forest
or the end of an argument.

Different to down there:
gas stations pumping smoke,
workers click-clacking at reports,
wrong lovers tangled beneath sheets,
the never-ending spin of earth.

Yes, different, because over there
the peaks of Y Garn & Crib Goch,
their red ridge summits rising to join me:
how long they must have climbed,
how many lessons on their way up

to this other world of sunlight
where air is thin yet easier to breathe
where a buzzard soars above the cloud

& the moon is white & full,
alone in this bed of blue.

Longing

For in this endless summer
where heat is thick to the
touch, fields yellowed &
parched,
it is easy, oh so easy,
to be longing

& walking the edgelands
of the river, moving out
from the city, as a lover
approaches the opposite way,
it is easy, oh so easy
to be longing

& upon meeting under bough
of an old english willow,
& not touching but stepping
into meadow pristine,
golden in the light
& abuzz with the season,
it is easy, oh so easy
to be longing

& so far from home
that the world
feels turned off
& the field & the sky

are a dreamscape
& the oak at the centre
so still as she moves
to its shade with a wave
& a sway in her walk,
it is easy, oh so easy,
to be longing.

Myosotis Sylvatica

I rip them from forest,
morning sun then evening shade,
two clusters of forget-me-nots,
newly sprung, greening
my pocket as I amble
the old pathway home.

Replanted,
they spiral
into base of soil,
charcoal, pebble,
surrounded
no longer by woodland
but glass globe terrarium,
hustle of living room,
& a bottle-top exit
way beyond their reach.

Slowly, they rise,
stems regaining strength
& in their move
towards sunlight
they colour & bloom,
stretching upward
into open air.

Oh how they must breathe
making their escape,
curling this way & that,
choosing to extend themselves
beyond glass cage,

perhaps return to the woodland
to dance beneath star
studded canopy
or nestle between rock cress,
male fern, tulip

or maybe simply
to wander to the river,
sit aside the jetty
& watch sun set
in a final flash
of golden pink.

The Crow

Where the waves curl in,
recede & leave mussel,
crab-claw & seaweed
scattered over sand,
a crow skulks,
grips a clam pincer-like
between her beak, opens
her wings & lifts
into the slipstream
of a cold north-westerly.

She hovers five metres or so
above the prom, drops
the shell, floats down
to inspect, collect, repeat
the process until the clam
peppers the concrete.

I watch from the bench
take note of her perseverance,
her attention to detail,
her patience & rhythm.

How she makes a meal
from beach & wind & shell.

Highland

Fur still matted from the slick
& slip of her long-night's labour,
this highland mother, weak-legged

& frail, steps to the edge of the pen;
moonlight caught on the wet of her nose,
her pupil reflecting the night.

Her snout brushes my hand.
There is a charge in the touch,
a tension to the mood.

I am sniffed out for threat.
My near-empty bottle of red
a cause for worry.

Settling now, her guard dropped,
she lets out a slow long sigh,
too tired to hold back her caution.

Tilting her head, she nestles
into my palm, drops her long-lashed eyes,
lets out another sigh

softer this time
welcoming the affection,
her head heavy at my palm.

Resting,
she holds me in her gaze,
holds a smile, a curiosity

for she sees in me my youth,
sees me drunk on more than just
Merlot & wonders about her own

whether they will ever
be granted the chance
to trot beneath midnight sky,

gallop frosted fields
for no other reason
than the fact

they are right there,
out in front,
calling our names.

Jungle

think Leeds Fest   monday morning

think of tents ripped & shelled
of poles protruding like steel from bombed buildings
of black smoke & the embers of forgotten fires
of blackened nails & unwashed hair
of bodies covered in sweat & grime & rain

think Leeds Fest   monday morning

remove the pick-up points filled with cars
the queues of parents waiting to rescue weary teens
the heat on full & McDonald's meals at the ready

think Leeds Fest   sunday evening

replace the flares of headline set
with flares that call for help
arms thrown up to basslines
with those thrown up in prayer

think Leeds Fest   monday morning

replace sunlit valley with ocean storm
with a pair of gloves passed round every half hour
with screams when the boat hits a wave

it was never built to manage
with t shirts soaked through, a body overboard,
your mother's jeans stained red at the crotch

replace the exit to the car park
with a barbed wire fence
manned by riot shields & helmets
placed there to keep you in
but most importantly
keep you out

think Leeds Fest   monday morning

think of it for a year
think about how you never thought
your journey would finish here
yet you haven't moved
& neither has the mud
& neither has the world

Regeneration

First from hibernation are the solar-powered lights.
Man-made & mortal, their single crystal circuits
are close to finished, ready for the scrap heap.

But with January sun coursing their systems,
they fight against the dark, mere glimmer
as they wake themselves from slumber.

Across their brittle mechanics,
sunlight streams, turns silver-white,
lights the skeleton tree, the city backyard

& for the first time in months
despite the last great bite of winter,
they are beacons in frosted soil.

The next morning, I light a cigarette
on this winter-bare terrace. I wait
for the warmth of sun upon my cheek.

Acknowledgements

Thanks are given to the editors of the following magazines and anthologies where some of these poems first appeared, in either their current form or an earlier shape: In The Red 15, Bloom, Independent Variable, 192.

My thanks also go to the Liverpool John Moores University Creative Writing department of 2018. To Helen Tookey, Sarah Maclennan, Jeff Young, Andrew McMillan & Seán Hewitt, your guidance and enthusiasm is a large part of why this pamphlet exists.

To Horatio Clare, your positivity for the world and its people, and the way you see and narrate your experiences is second to none. Without realising, your way of being has had a huge inspiration on all the writing and reading I undertake.

To Erik and my parents, words can do no justice, but thank you for your ever present support, feedback and general ways of being.

To Jessica and her jetty – we came so close. Thank you for everything.